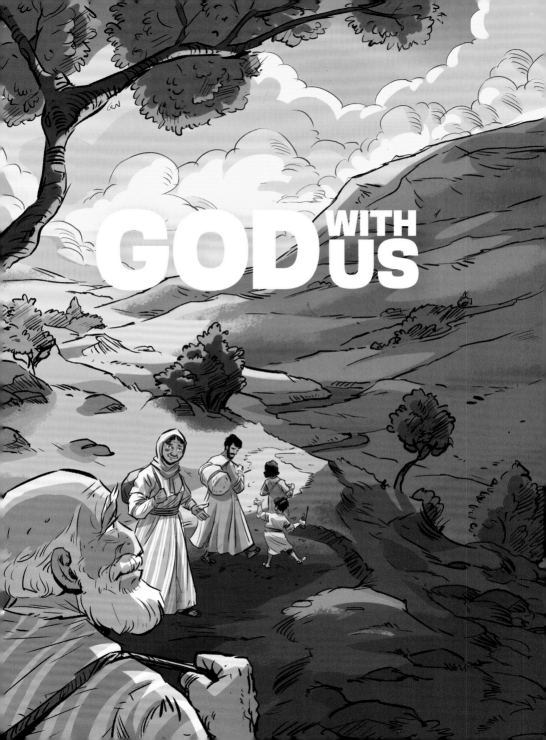

GOD WITH US

BIBLE STORIES ON THE ROAD TO EMMAUS

Written by
Matt Mikalatos

Illustrated by
David Shephard

Foreword by
Renjy Abraham
of BibleProject

Colored by
Whitney Cogar

WATERBROOK

To Joe Field, the owner of Flying Colors Comics & Other Cool Stuff, and to his lovely family. Blessings and peace to you.

—Matt

In memory of Dave Shephard, whose art continues to delight and move us.

Text copyright © 2025 by Matt Mikalatos
Cover art and interior illustrations copyright © 2025 by the Estate of David Shephard
Foreword by Renjy Abraham copyright © 2025 by Penguin Random House LLC

Hardback ISBN 978-0-593-57810-0
Ebook ISBN 978-0-593-57811-7

The Library of Congress catalog record is available at https://lccn.loc.gov/2024043170.

Printed in China

waterbrookmultnomah.com

10 9 8 7 6 5 4 3 2 1

First Edition

Letterer: Sam Migliore
Designers: Bones Leopard and Sonia Persad
Editor: Sarah Rubio
Publisher: Laura Barker
Production Editor: Laura K. Wright
Copy Editor: Tracey Moore
Proofreaders: Bailey Utecht, Michael Fedison, Carrie Krause, and JoLeigh Buchanan
Managing Editor: Julia Wallace
Production Manager: Linnea Knollmueller

Contents

Foreword

This graphic novel by Matt Mikalatos illuminates the ancient world, weaving modern imagery together with biblical scenes and inviting us to see ourselves within one of the New Testament's most mysterious moments. Somehow, Jesus conceals his identity as he walks with grieving travelers who are confused over his death. In the Bible, this story is brief but packed with irony and dense symbolism that Matt opens and fleshes out, exploring the story's implications with creative imagination. He combines careful scholarship with David Shephard's beautiful artwork to set us on the dusty first-century path with Jesus and his companions as they journey toward Emmaus.

I love the comic medium because it's a fun and disarming way to invite people to engage with the Scriptures. When we open this sacred book, we travel to an ancient world pulsing with life and energy. Yet, for some, the Bible's ancient context can be a hindrance. Its foreignness makes it appear strange and difficult to interact with and understand. For others, the Bible is all too familiar, which breeds complacency. These stories can become stale and zap our curiosity. But this graphic novel will cultivate reflection and spark wonder in every reader. You'll be taken aback in the best way by Matt's creative approach, which will enliven characters and forge empathic pathways. The comic-style art captures emotions in more profound ways than words alone.

The Emmaus Road narrative is a beautiful passage to spend time with because its allusions and twists invite us to explore the overarching story of the Hebrew Bible (also known as the Old Testament). Though the Scriptures can seem like a series of disconnected stories, poems, prophecies, and instructions, they are more like an interconnected quilt of various materials from different origins that all work together. Ancient scribes stitched these pieces into their final form to express an inspired and unified story that points to a person. As you will find in this graphic novel, Jesus claims that this epic story all leads to him. If you've never engaged with the Emmaus Road story, hang on for an adventure.

Matt carefully and creatively guides us on this journey with Jesus, making his way through the Old Testament stories to communicate ancient wisdom in a fresh way. I have known Matt for more than two decades, and I have experienced the warmth, joy, and hope you will encounter in these pages. *God with Us* offers a vibrant telling of a sacred story and welcomes us to discover something new on the Road to Emmaus.

—Renjy Abraham
Dean of Scholarship,
BibleProject

Introduction

Comic books and the Bible have a lot in common. Pretty much every kind of story you like comes in comic form. There are funny comics, cowboy comics, mystery comics, romance comics, superhero comics (duh), science fiction comics—you name it. The Bible has all kinds of stories too. There are funny stories, like the one with the guy who is supposed to speak up for God but won't, so God sends a fish to eat him (and then puke him up). There are adventure stories and stories that are pure history and romances, like Ruth and Boaz, and amazing superhero-type stories, like the one with the guy who is so strong he can tear down a temple with his bare hands! Pretty much any kind of story you like, the Bible has a story like that.

There are monsters and heroes and spies and warriors and talking animals and queens. Sometimes people come back from the dead. There are wolves and bears and snakes and cute little sheep. There are miracles, like walking on water or feeding a gigantic crowd with a kid's lunch.

One story I love takes place after Jesus died. Two of his friends are walking down the road when Jesus shows up, but they don't recognize him. Jesus starts telling them all these stories from the Bible and explains that even the oldest ones—like how God created the world—were about the Savior who was to come, Jesus.

The Bible doesn't tell us which stories Jesus told his friends that day. But I thought, wouldn't it be fun to imagine which stories they were and how Jesus might have told them? That's the idea behind this book. Parts of this book come straight out of the Bible. For instance, we know that one of the people walking down the road with Jesus was a guy named Cleopas. We have to make some guesses about who the other person was. A lot of Bible teachers think it was Cleopas's wife, Mary (or Miriam).

There are other details I made up, but I always added them to help us get closer to the Bible story and see it clearly. Moshe and Rachel are completely imagined, but I think you'll like them and how they interact with Jesus (called by his Hebrew name, Yeshua, in this book!). Were there really kids on the road with Jesus? Probably! Lots of travelers, including families and friends, walked the road together.

Our talented artist, Dave Shephard, and I also wanted to give you some fun peeks into what it would have been like to walk around with Jesus. Dave worked hard to make the land and trees and bushes, buildings, furniture, clothes (and toys!) look close to how they would have in those days. Dave also did an amazing job bringing all the characters to life, and I enjoy seeing Yeshua as he eats and talks and laughs alongside the other people in this book. I'm sad to say that Dave passed away before we were done with this project. I am so thankful for his partnership in bringing this book into being. I'm also thankful for Whitney Cogar, who stepped in and did just a spectacular job with the beautiful colors in this book.

I love comics, and I love the Bible. I hope this graphic novel makes you love the Bible more too. Happy reading and have fun!

— **Matt Mikalatos**

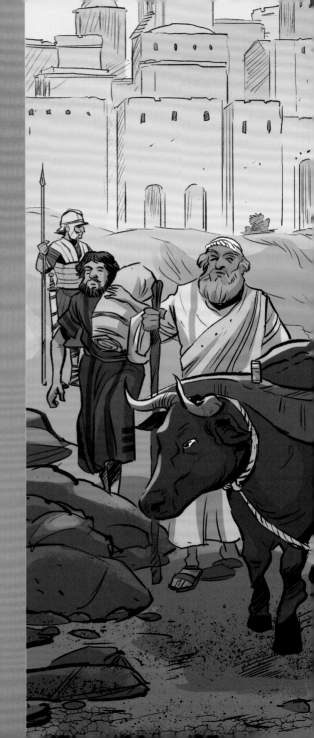

CHAPTER 1

BEGINNINGS

DEATH, DANGER, FRIENDS IN HIDING... I'D CERTAINLY LIKE TO HEAR MORE.

WHAT THINGS?

YOU MUST BE THE ONLY PERSON IN ALL OF JERUSALEM NOT TO KNOW THESE THINGS.

WHAT HAPPENED TO YESHUA!

YESHUA OF NAZARETH.

YOU'VE NEVER HEARD OF HIM? HA HA!

MOSHE, SHH! SHOW SOME RESPECT.

LEAVE ME ALONE, RACHEL!

TELL ME.

HOW FOOLISH YOU ARE.

AND HOW SLOW OF HEART TO BELIEVE THE PROPHETS.

DIDN'T THE SAVIOR OF THE WORLD HAVE TO SUFFER THESE THINGS AND THEN ENTER HIS GLORY?

COME BACK!

WHAT ARE YOU TALKING ABOUT?

DO YOU WANT ME TO TELL YOU THE STORY?

YES!

LET'S START AT THE BEGINNING, THEN.

GOD'S WORK WAS DONE ON DAY SEVEN, SO GOD INVENTED REST.

GOD BLESSED THE SEVENTH DAY. IT IS A HOLY DAY, BECAUSE ON THAT DAY GOD RESTED FROM THE WORK OF CREATION.

I DON'T THINK YOU TOLD THAT RIGHT.

IT'S NOT WRONG, BUT I'VE NEVER HEARD IT LIKE THAT.

THAT STORY REMINDS ME...

...OF SOMETHING YESHUA'S MOTHER SAID.

ABOUT WHEN GOD SPOKE TO HER.

"LET THERE BE LIGHT." I NEVER THOUGHT OF IT THAT WAY. THE WORD...

THE WORD OF GOD.

NOTHING SPECIAL.

MARY SAID IT WAS AN ORDINARY DAY. NOTHING HOLY ABOUT IT.

20

GOD SAID, "LET THERE BE LIGHT," AND THERE WAS. AND GOD SPOKE LIFE INTO MARY'S WOMB, AND THERE WAS!

I NEVER THOUGHT OF IT THAT WAY...

SO... YESHUA DIDN'T HAVE A DAD?

HUH. MOM AND DAD DIDN'T TELL ME THIS PART.

OF COURSE YESHUA HAD A FATHER! GOD WAS HIS FATHER, AND A MAN NAMED JOSEPH ADOPTED HIM TOO.

SPEAKING OF YOUR PARENTS, WHERE ARE THEY?

I WOULD BE IN SO MUCH TROUBLE IF I HAD A DAD ON EARTH AND ONE IN HEAVEN WATCHING MY EVERY MOVE.

GOD HAS A WAY OF BRINGING LIGHT WHERE WE THINK THERE CAN ONLY BE DARKNESS.

AND LIFE...

...WHERE WE WOULDN'T EXPECT TO FIND IT.

AND THE MAN BECAME A LIVING SOUL!

HOLD ON. SO YOU'RE SAYING GOD COULD TURN THIS ROCK INTO A PERSON?

OF COURSE.

THAT WOULD BE A VERY SMALL PERSON.

GO ON, MISTER. GOD MADE THE MAN, AND THEN...

I THINK...

HE SAW A VISION.

GOD TOLD HIM HE'S GOING TO GROW WINGS?

GO FIND ELIZABETH.

A WORD THAT BRINGS LIFE WHERE WE WOULD NOT EXPECT IT.

JUST LIKE MARY, ZECHARIAH WAS SUPPOSED TO GIVE HIS BABY A SPECIAL NAME.

LIKE THE MAN NAMED THE ANIMALS!

AND HOW GABRIEL SPOKE TO MARY TOO!

THE PEOPLE WALKING IN DARKNESS SAW A GREAT LIGHT!

GOD BRINGS LIFE IN PLACES WHERE LIFE SEEMS IMPOSSIBLE.

SHE'S NOT DEAD. SHE'S SLEEPING.

LITTLE GIRL, GET UP.

THE LORD BRINGS LIGHT WHERE THERE WAS ONLY DARKNESS.

LORD, I HAVE BEEN BLIND SINCE I WAS A CHILD.

I CAN SEE. I CAN SEE!

LIFE WHERE LIFE CAN'T BE ... THAT'S WHAT GOD DOES.

HE'S NOT HERE!

WHERE COULD HE BE?

35

Glory to God!

I sing from the depths of my soul, because he noticed me—a little nobody.

He saw me and thought of me! Everyone will say how blessed I am!

The Mighty God—the Holy One—has done wonderful things for me. If we show God respect, he shows us mercy. That was true for our grandparents, and it will be true for our grandchildren.

People who are full of themselves—God sends them running. He pulls rulers down off their high thrones, and he lifts up lowly poor folks. He feeds hungry people with delicious food, but he sends rich people away with nothing.

He helps Israel and has shown us mercy . . . just like he promised! He always keeps his promises, because his Word shapes the world!

THREE MONTHS LATER, JUST WHEN MARY'S OWN BABY STARTED TO SHOW, ELIZABETH WENT INTO LABOR.

WHAT'S HIS NAME?

JOHN.

JOHN? BUT THAT'S NOT ONE OF YOUR FAMILY NAMES!

THE NAME MEANS "GOD'S GRACE." I LIKE IT.

HOW COULD SUCH OLD PEOPLE HAVE A BABY?

CLAP CLAP

Praise God, who is coming to save his people. God told us salvation would come through David, and the Lord has done it!

He has saved us from our enemies! Saved us from those who hate us! The Lord has shown us mercy!

The Lord promised Abraham that God would rescue us, would give us power to serve the Lord without fear in holiness and right action for the rest of our days!

And you, my boy, John!

You will be called the spokesman of the Most High. You'll walk ahead of the Lord and make things ready for the Savior of the world. You'll tell people how to be saved, how to be forgiven, because our God is tender and merciful.

"... TO GUIDE US ONTO THE PATH OF PEACE."

THAT'S NOT THE END OF THE STORY, IS IT?

WHAT ABOUT ADAM AND THE SNAKE? WHAT ABOUT MOSES AND DAVID AND RUTH AND ALL OF THEM?

WE'VE KNOWN THESE STORIES SINCE WE WERE CHILDREN.

AND YET THEY SEEM ... NEW.

CITIZENS OF HEAVEN BRING NEW TREASURES OUT OF OLD STOREROOMS.

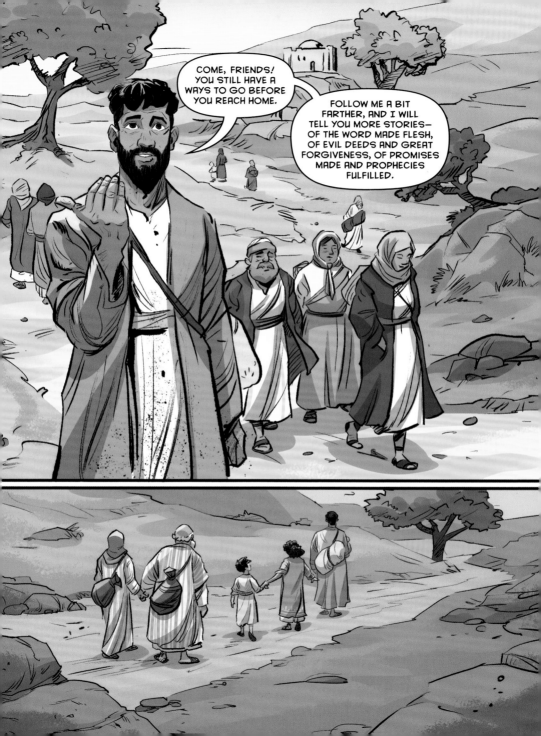

CHAPTER 2

BROKEN

48

THIS IS A BIG MISTAKE!

THE WOMAN'S HUSBAND, WHO WAS STANDING RIGHT THERE, ATE SOME TOO. THEY DIDN'T DIE...

BUT THEIR EYES WERE OPENED, AND THEY REALIZED THEY WERE NAKED.

AND THE LORD GOD SAID, "WE CAN'T ALLOW HUMANITY TO EAT FROM THE TREE OF LIFE AND LIVE FOREVER. THEY MUST BE BANISHED FROM THE GARDEN."

GOD PLACED AN ANGEL TO PROTECT THE WAY TO THE TREE OF LIFE.

THE MAN NAMED THE WOMAN HAVAH,* "TO BREATHE" OR "TO LIVE," FOR SHE WOULD BECOME THE MOTHER OF ALL THE LIVING.

*HAVAH IS OFTEN TRANSLATED AS "EVE."

HOW STRANGE THAT GOD WOULD BAR THE WAY TO ETERNAL LIFE. AND YET . . .

YESHUA OFFERED LIFE FREELY.

IF YOU ARE THIRSTY, COME AND DRINK! IF YOU BELIEVE IN ME, STREAMS OF LIVING WATER WILL OVERFLOW FROM YOUR HEARTS!

TELL ME, MA'AM, DID NO ONE CONDEMN YOU?

NO ONE, SIR.

THEN I DON'T CONDEMN YOU EITHER.

GO HOME. AND DON'T BREAK GOD'S LAWS AGAIN.

THAT STORY DOESN'T MAKE SENSE.

MOSHE, YOU LOVE TO BE FORGIVEN WHEN YOU MESS UP.

SWING

PEOPLE WHO BREAK THE LAW MUST BE PUNISHED!

STOP!

GIVE IT BACK!

SWIPE

I'M SO SORRY! I DIDN'T MEAN TO—

THROUGH THE WATERS

GOD TOLD NOAH WHAT SIZE TO BUILD IT, HOW TO CUT CYPRESS WOOD, HOW TO WATERPROOF WITH PITCH, AND HOW MUCH FOOD TO BRING.

SEVEN DAYS BEFORE THE RAIN, GOD SENT ANIMALS: SEVEN PAIRS EACH OF "CLEAN" ANIMALS—GOOD FOR EATING AND SACRIFICES—AND ONE PAIR EACH OF "UNCLEAN" ANIMALS.

GOD SHUT THE DOOR.

THEN HE OPENED GREAT SPRINGS BENEATH THE EARTH AND THE FLOODGATES OF HEAVEN. IT RAINED NONSTOP FOR 40 DAYS AND NIGHTS.

EVEN THE MOUNTAINS WERE FLOODED.

EVERYTHING DIED. EVERYTHING.

ONLY NOAH AND HIS FAMILY AND THE ANIMALS IN THE BOAT WERE LEFT.

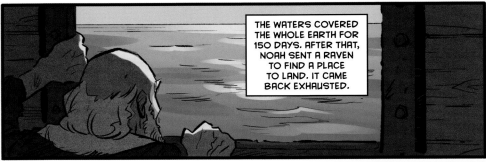

THE WATERS COVERED THE WHOLE EARTH FOR 150 DAYS. AFTER THAT, NOAH SENT A RAVEN TO FIND A PLACE TO LAND. IT CAME BACK EXHAUSTED.

THEN HE SENT A DOVE, WHICH CAME BACK WITH AN OLIVE LEAF! THE WATER WAS DRAINING AWAY!

IT WAS A FRESH START FOR EVERYONE.

NOAH MADE A SACRIFICE TO GOD.

GOD WAS PLEASED AND SAID . . .

EVEN IF HUMANS ONLY THINK ABOUT WICKED THINGS FOREVER

I'LL NEVER DESTROY EVERY LIVING THING AGAIN.

SO LONG AS THE EARTH EXISTS, THERE WILL BE A TIME TO PLANT AND A TIME TO HARVEST, COLD TIMES AND HOT TIMES, BOTH SUMMER AND WINTER, NIGHT AND DAY. ALL THESE THINGS WILL GO ON SO LONG AS THE EARTH DOES.

GOD BLESSED THEM AND TOLD THEM TO FILL THE EARTH. HE SAID VIOLENCE AGAINST HUMAN BEINGS MUST ALWAYS BE PUNISHED.

GOD MADE A COVENANT, A BINDING PROMISE, WITH EVERY PERSON AND EVERY ANIMAL.

NO MATTER HOW BAD HUMANITY GETS . . .

I WILL NEVER FLOOD THE EARTH AGAIN.

LOOK, I'LL SHOW YOU I'M SERIOUS. THIS IS MY WAR BOW. I'M SETTING IT ASIDE FOREVER. I'M PLACING IT IN THE SKY WHERE YOU CAN SEE IT.

NO MORE WILL THERE BE WAR BETWEEN GOD AND HUMANITY.

DON'T YOU THINK THE BODIES STANK, CLEOPAS?

I SUPPOSE THEY DID.

WHAT IS IT, DEAR? YOU SEEM DISTRACTED.

YEAH! YOU DIDN'T EVEN IGNORE MOSHE'S TERRIBLE QUESTION.

HEY!

SOMETHING ABOUT THAT STORY . . .

ABOUT HOW NOAH WAS SAVED AND CAME THROUGH THE WATER. AND THE DOVE. WHY DOES THAT SEEM SO IMPORTANT?

I REMEMBER A DOVE STORY. WITH THE TEACHER, YESHUA, RIGHT?

THAT'S IT, RACHEL, YES! I'M THINKING OF JOHN THE BAPTIZER.

WHO THE WHAT NOW?

JOHN THE BAPTIZER! HE LIVED OUTSIDE THE CITY.

HE DRESSED IN CAMEL HAIR AND ATE LOCUSTS AND WILD HONEY.

YUCK.

THIS STORY IS MAKING ME HUNGRY.

YES! AND HE TAUGHT THE PEOPLE THEY NEEDED TO STOP DOING WHAT WAS WRONG AND TURN TO GOD.

IS THIS ZECHARIAH AND ELIZABETH'S BABY? YESHUA'S COUSIN?

DO YOU HAVE TWO SHIRTS? SHARE ONE.

DO YOU HAVE FOOD? THEN SPLIT IT WITH THOSE WHO HAVE NONE.

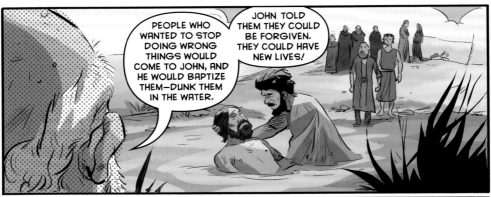

PEOPLE WHO WANTED TO STOP DOING WRONG THINGS WOULD COME TO JOHN, AND HE WOULD BAPTIZE THEM—DUNK THEM IN THE WATER.

JOHN TOLD THEM THEY COULD BE FORGIVEN. THEY COULD HAVE NEW LIVES!

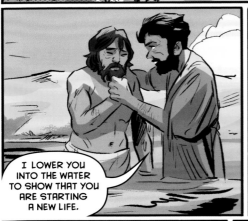

I LOWER YOU INTO THE WATER TO SHOW THAT YOU ARE STARTING A NEW LIFE.

WHEN THE SAVIOR COMES, HE WILL BAPTIZE YOU IN FIRE!

I REMEMBER THIS. SOMETHING TERRIBLE HAPPENS TO JOHN!

NOT YET, DEAR HEART. FIRST, SOMETHING WONDERFUL HAPPENS.

BUT ONE SHALL COME WHOSE SANDALS I AM NOT WORTHY EVEN TO UNTIE!

AND A VOICE FROM HEAVEN SAID... WHAT DID IT SAY AGAIN, MIRIAM?

"THIS IS MY SON. I LOVE HIM, AND I'M PLEASED WITH HIM."

WAIT...WERE YOU *THERE* WHEN YESHUA WAS BAPTIZED?

YES, BUT EVEN THEN I DIDN'T RECOGNIZE THIS!

HUMANITY WAS SAVED BY NOAH'S TRIP THROUGH THE WATER, AND YESHUA DID THE SAME THING. AND THE DOVE!

AFTER THE FLOOD, GOD SAID WE'RE NOT AT WAR ANYMORE.

GOD SAID THERE WOULD BE ANOTHER WAY TO DEAL WITH OUR SINS.

NOAH IS A STORY ABOUT THE WORLD BEING SAVED FROM DESTRUCTION, AND SO IS THE STORY OF YESHUA!

BUT WHAT OF THE SACRIFICE, HMM?

YOUR LITTLE BAPTISM STORY IS INTERESTING, BUT GOD REQUIRES SACRIFICE.

NOAH AND YESHUA WENT THROUGH THE WATER. THEY BOTH SAW THE DOVE. SO WHAT?

I AM ITZHAK BEN SIMEON, A PHARISEE AND RELIGIOUS RULER.

I DO NOT USUALLY SPEND MY TIME TEACHING CHILDREN.

NOBODY ASKED YOU TO.

I CAN SEE SOMEONE HAS FILLED YOUR HEAD WITH INACCURATE TEACHINGS, AND SINCE IT WOULD PASS THE TIME ON THE ROAD . . .

MY LAST THREE HEBREW TEACHERS QUIT.

IT'S DECIDED. I SHALL WALK WITH YOU A WAYS AND TEACH YOU BETTER THINGS.

WHAT DID I MISS?

CLEOPAS AND MIRIAM TOLD US ABOUT YESHUA'S BAPTISM.

AND THEN THIS GUY SHOWED UP, AND NOW HE'S GOING TO GIVE A LECTURE.

ALL RESPECT TO YOU, RABBI. MAY I LISTEN TO YOUR LECTURE?

I SEE NO HARM IN YOUR JOINING US.

CHILDREN, TRY TO KEEP UP.

WHERE IS BAAZ?

HE GOT SOME GOOD NEWS AND HURRIED OFF TO SHARE IT WITH HIS LOVED ONES.

BUT COME. I AM EAGER TO HEAR WHAT ITZHAK HAS TO SAY.

THAT MAKES ONE OF US.

CHAPTER 4

THE LAW OF SACRIFICE

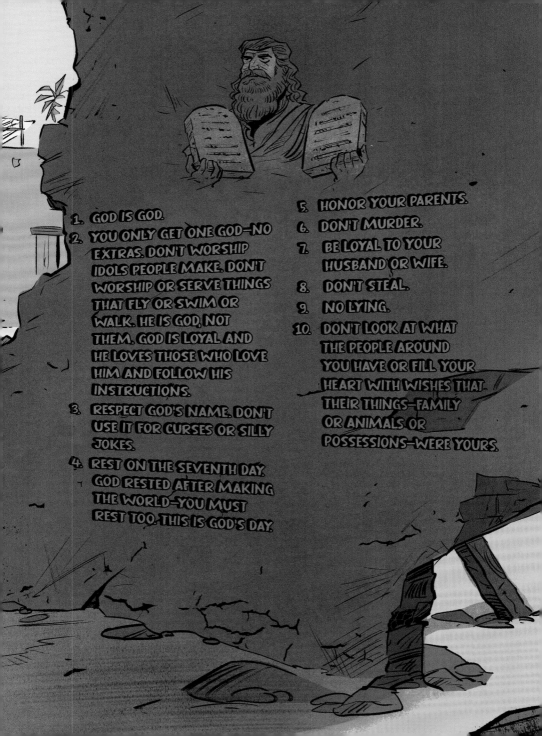

DO YOU KNOW THE MOST FAMOUS STORY OF SACRIFICE?

JEPHTHAH?

I'M THINKING OF SOMEONE WITH MY OWN NAME.

ISAAC!

YES! HIS FATHER, ABRAHAM, WAS AN OLD MAN WHEN GOD SAID, "YOUR DESCENDANTS WILL BE AS MANY AS THE STARS IN THE SKY."

GOD GAVE HIM A SON. WHEN ABRAHAM WAS OLDER STILL, GOD SAID TO HIM . . .

"TAKE YOUR ONLY SON, WHOM YOU LOVE, TO A MOUNTAIN I'LL SHOW YOU. KILL THE BOY AS A HUMAN SACRIFICE . . . TO PROVE YOU ARE MY FOLLOWER."

I HATE THIS STORY. RACHEL, HOLD ME!

IT'LL BE OKAY, MOSHE.

FATHER, YOU FORGOT THE LAMB FOR THE SACRIFICE.

IS YOUR POINT THAT DAVID MADE A SACRIFICE AND GOD REWARDED HIM?

WHAT DID DAVID SAY ABOUT THAT DAY?

IT'S GOD WHO SAVES THE DAY, NOT MIGHTY WARRIORS.

YESHUA SPENT TIME WITH PEOPLE WHO DID EVERYTHING WRONG. SINNERS AND TAX COLLECTORS . . .

YOU SHOULDN'T BE WITH THOSE SINNERS!

THAT'S LIKE SAYING A DOCTOR SHOULDN'T BE WITH THE SICK. GOD SAYS . . .

I DESIRE MERCY, NOT SACRIFICE.

HMM. MERCY, NOT SACRIFICE.

WHEN MESSIAH—SAVIOR OF THE WORLD—COMES, HE'LL EXPLAIN EVERYTHING.

THAT'S ME.

YOU THINK MESSIAH WOULD TELL A SAMARITAN WHO HE WAS BEFORE TELLING MORE WORTHY PEOPLE?

WHO DO YOU THINK HE SHOULD TELL . . . YOU?!

HOW LOW HAVE I FALLEN? I'M ARGUING WITH CHILDREN!

YESHUA IS SAYING THAT BEING CONNECTED TO GOD'S SPIRIT IS MORE IMPORTANT THAN FIGHTING OVER RULES.

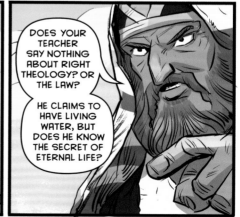

DOES YOUR TEACHER SAY NOTHING ABOUT RIGHT THEOLOGY? OR THE LAW?

HE CLAIMS TO HAVE LIVING WATER, BUT DOES HE KNOW THE SECRET OF ETERNAL LIFE?

111

IS HE YOUR RELATIVE THAT YOU WOULD CARE FOR HIM THIS WAY?

NOT AT ALL. I ONLY WANT HIM TO GET BETTER.

ITZHAK, WHICH OF THE THREE MEN WAS A NEIGHBOR TO THE MAN WHO WAS ROBBED?

THE ONE WHO SHOWED THE MAN MERCY.

IT WAS THE—

BUT HE ISN'T—

HE'S NOT—

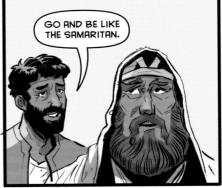

GO AND BE LIKE THE SAMARITAN.

I GUESS HE'S DONE TEACHING US?

I'VE HEARD THAT STORY BEFORE.

I HEARD IT TOO—FROM YESHUA.

TEACHER, CAN I ASK A QUESTION?

OF COURSE, RACHEL.

YOU SAID THAT TO LIVE FOREVER WITH GOD, WE MUST LOVE GOD AND OTHERS. BUT THE SAMARITAN DIDN'T BELIEVE LIKE WE DO.

HOW CAN YOU TELL A FIG TREE FROM AN OLIVE TREE?

CHAPTER 5

DAILY BREAD

STEW!

NO, DATES!

CHEESE!

MY HUSBAND WAS A PROPHET AND HAS LEFT US WITH NOTHING. MY CREDITORS THREATEN TO TAKE MY BOYS!

PLEASE HELP!

WHAT DO YOU HAVE IN YOUR HOUSE?

A SMALL JAR OF OLIVE OIL, NOTHING MORE.

TAKE THE BOYS AND GO TO YOUR NEIGHBORS.

"ASK THEM FOR ALL THEIR EMPTY JARS."

"GO INTO YOUR HOUSE AND CLOSE THE DOORS."

"AND POUR YOUR OLIVE OIL."

GOD TOOK CARE OF THE WIDOW AND HER SONS.

WHY DIDN'T HE JUST GIVE THEM MONEY?

YESHUA PERFORMED A MIRACLE MUCH LIKE THIS ONE.

IS THAT SO?

AT A DIFFICULT TIME TOO.

HIS COUSIN JOHN HAD JUST BEEN KILLED.

YESHUA WAS DEEPLY WOUNDED BY THE LOSS.

THE BAPTIZER GUY?

ELIZABETH'S SON.

HE TOLD HIS FOLLOWERS...

LET'S GET AWAY FOR A WHILE.

TAKE THE BOAT AND GO WHERE NO ONE CAN FIND US.

BUT THE CROWDS HEARD YESHUA WAS IN THE BOAT AND RAN TO THE OTHER SIDE OF THE LAKE TO WAIT FOR HIM.

TEACHER, DO YOU WANT TO FIND ANOTHER PLACE TO GET AWAY?

HE SAW THEM AND FELT ONLY COMPASSION.

THEY'RE LOST AND HELPLESS, LIKE SHEEP WITHOUT A SHEPHERD.

HE HEALED THE SICK . . .

AND TAUGHT ABOUT GOD'S KINGDOM.

A MAN FOUND A PRICELESS TREASURE IN A FIELD AND SOLD EVERYTHING TO BUY THE FIELD.

HE WAS THRILLED AT THE GREAT PRICE!

SOME OF THE PEOPLE WANTED TO OVERTHROW THE GOVERNMENT AND MAKE YESHUA KING!

BUT YESHUA KNEW WHAT THEY WERE THINKING. HE SLIPPED AWAY SO NO ONE COULD FIND HIM.

WOULDN'T MAKING HIM KING BE GOOD, THOUGH?

ISN'T THAT WHAT WE MEAN WHEN WE SAY GOD'S KINGDOM IS COMING?

YESHUA DID SAY SOMETHING LIKE THAT. HIS FOLLOWERS HAD ASKED HIM . . .

LORD, TEACH US TO PRAY!

"SOME PEOPLE MAKE A BIG SPECTACLE WHEN THEY'RE PRAYING, WANTING TO MAKE SURE EVERYONE SEES THEM. PEOPLE'S ATTENTION IS ALL THEY GET."

WHEN YOU PRAY ALONE IN YOUR ROOM, GOD HEARS YOU. GOD WILL ANSWER!

GOD KNOWS WHAT YOU NEED—YOU DON'T HAVE TO SAY IT OVER AND OVER.

PRAYER ISN'T A MAGIC SPELL.

WHEN YOU PRAY, DO IT SOMETHING LIKE THIS...

Our Father, who fills the whole universe
and is as near as the air we breathe,
may your name be treasured and treated
with the proper respect.

We want you to be King here on Earth,
and for this to be your kingdom. May the things
that you want done, be done here on Earth
just like it is already in Heaven.

Please give us the things we need
to get through the day.
Forgive us our wrongs against you,
just like we forgive those who wrong us.

Please don't put us through trials,
and protect us from every evil thing. Because
you are the one in charge, and you have all
the power and the glory, forever!

And that's exactly the way we want it to be.

LIKE RUTH.

SHE WAS A FOREIGNER WHO MARRIED A HEBREW.

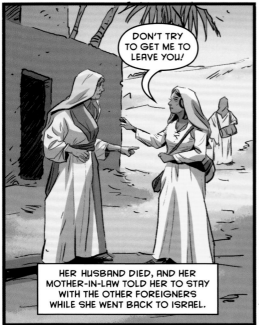

DON'T TRY TO GET ME TO LEAVE YOU!

HER HUSBAND DIED, AND HER MOTHER-IN-LAW TOLD HER TO STAY WITH THE OTHER FOREIGNERS WHILE SHE WENT BACK TO ISRAEL.

WHERE YOU GO, I'LL GO. YOUR PEOPLE WILL BE MY PEOPLE, AND YOUR GOD, MY GOD. WHERE YOU DIE, I'LL DIE, AND I'LL BE BURIED NEXT TO YOU.

MAY THE LORD PUNISH ME SEVERELY IF ANYTHING OTHER THAN DEATH SPLITS US UP.

IN TIME, RUTH MET A MAN OF ISRAEL NAMED BOAZ.

HIS NAME IS OBED.

AND THEY WERE MARRIED AND HAD A SON.

WAAAAIT A MINUTE. I KNOW THAT NAME.

OBED ALSO HAD A SON! HIS NAME WAS JESSE.

AND ONE DAY JESSE HAD SOME KIDS TOO!

THEY GROW UP SO FAST!

ELIAB

ABINADAB

SHIMEA

ZERUIAH

RADDAI

OZEM

ABIGAIL

NETHANEL

AND LIL DAVID.

LIL *KING* DAVID?!

YES! RUTH WAS HIS GREAT-GRANDMA.

RUTH IS AN ANCESTOR OF THE MESSIAH?!

THE SAVIOR OF THE WORLD IS A DESCENDANT OF DAVID.

YES! IMAGINE A GREAT BANQUET. A FEAST!

GO ON . . .

A WEALTHY MAN PLANNED IT, AND PEOPLE AGREED TO COME.

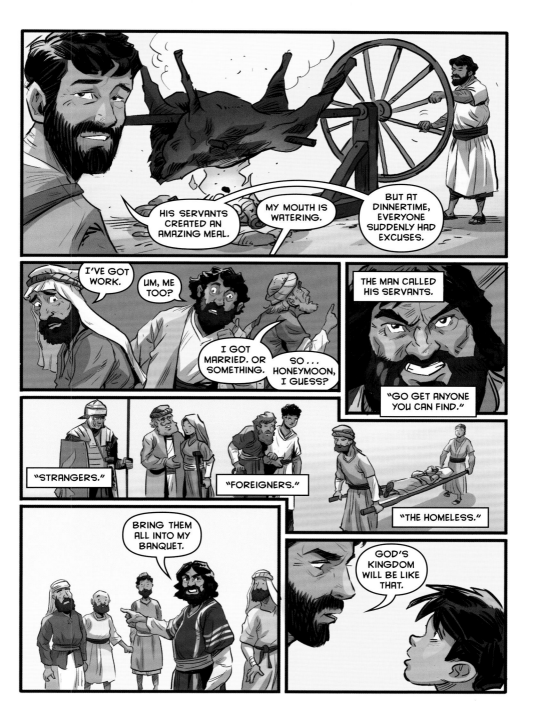

135

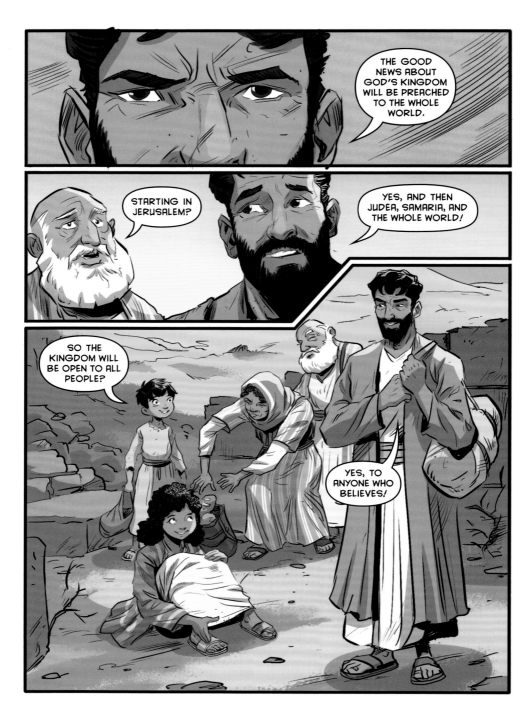

CHAPTER 6

THE BELLY
OF THE BEAST

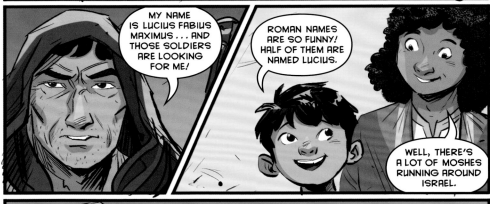

140

MOVE TO THE SIDE SO WE CAN TALK. I'LL KEEP AN EYE ON THE SOLDIERS.

MIRIAM IS WISE . . . SHE KNOWS I'M ABOUT TO TELL A STORY.

I HOPED THAT YOU WOULD, TEACHER!

THE WORD OF GOD CAME TO JONAH.

GET UP RIGHT NOW, AND GO TO NINEVEH.

TELL THEM THEIR EVIL STINKS SO BADLY I CAN SMELL IT FROM HEAVEN.

THEY HAVE MY ATTENTION, AND NOT IN A GOOD WAY.

SO JONAH, THE PROPHET— GOD'S SPOKESPERSON, GOD'S MESSENGER, THE MOUTHPIECE FOR GOD'S WORD—HASTILY PACKED A BAG AND RAN TO CATCH A BOAT.

GOD TOLD A BIG FISH, "GO SWALLOW MY SO-CALLED PROPHET, WHO DOESN'T DO WHAT HE'S TOLD."
AND THE FISH FOLLOWED GOD'S INSTRUCTIONS TO THE LETTER.
I REGRET MY LIFE CHOICES!
AS FOR THE SAILORS, THE STORM STOPPED RIGHT AWAY, AND THEY BECAME FOLLOWERS OF GOD.

THAT WAS A CLOSE ONE, GOD! I SHOUTED TOWARD YOU!
I WAS NERVOUS, BUT GOD HEARD ME. I HAD ONE FOOT,
MAYBE TWO FEET, IN THE GRAVE. I STARTED SHOUTING FROM
THE CENTER OF THIS TOMB AND YOU HEARD MY VOICE.

YOU HURLED ME INTO THE DEEP END INTO THE HEART OF
THE SEA. FLOODS OF WATER SURROUNDED ME! YOUR
BREAKERS AND YOUR WAVES CROSSED OVER ME.

I SAID TO MYSELF, "WELL, SELF, WE FINALLY DID IT.
WE MANAGED TO GET AWAY FROM GOD. OUT OF SIGHT.
I GUESS THIS IS IT. I WON'T SEE GOD OR THE TEMPLE IN
JERUSALEM OR BE IN GOD'S PRESENCE EVER AGAIN."

THE WATER ROSE UP TO MY CHIN AND I COULDN'T
TOUCH BOTTOM. THE ABYSS SURROUNDED ME
COMPLETELY. I WORE SEAWEED INSTEAD OF A HAT.

I SANK DOWN TO THE ROOTS OF THE MOUNTAINS.
THE GATES OF THE AFTERLIFE CLANGED SHUT BEHIND
ME, TRAPPING ME FOREVER, BUT YOU SNATCHED MY LIFE
UP FROM THE PIT OF DEATH. OH MY LORD! MY GOD!

MY SOUL WAS FAINTING AWAY FROM MY
BODY. BUT YOU NOTICED ME. MY PRAYERS
ENTERED INTO YOUR SACRED TEMPLE.

THOSE WHO REGARD THE WORTHLESSNESS OF
NOTHINGNESS, WHO PAY ATTENTION TO IDOLS,
ABANDON BOTH THEIR LOYALTY AND YOUR MERCY!

BUT AS FOR ME, I PROMISE TO SPEAK UP AND
USE MY VOICE TO SHOUT YOUR PRAISES.
I'M DEFINITELY GOING TO KEEP MY PROMISE. THE
ONLY ONE WHO CAN SAVE ME IS THE LORD!

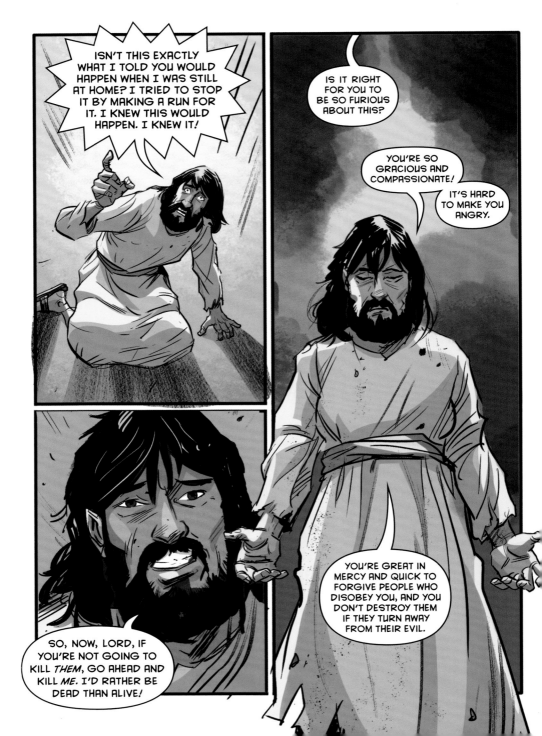

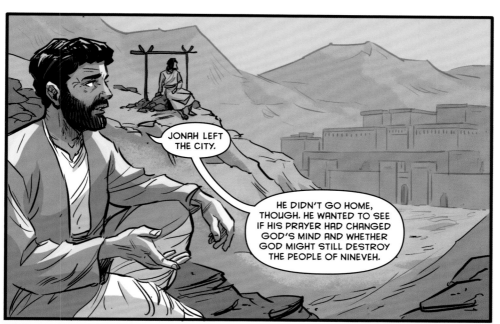

JONAH LEFT THE CITY.

HE DIDN'T GO HOME, THOUGH. HE WANTED TO SEE IF HIS PRAYER HAD CHANGED GOD'S MIND AND WHETHER GOD MIGHT STILL DESTROY THE PEOPLE OF NINEVEH.

GOD SENT A LITTLE PLANT TO GROW OVER JONAH'S HEAD, LIKE A LEAFY HAT—

A BIT OF SHADE TO RESCUE HIM FROM HIS MISERY AND HIS EVIL ATTITUDE.

JONAH WAS DELIRIOUSLY HAPPY ABOUT THE PLANT.

BUT THEN GOD ALSO SENT A WORM TO EAT THE PLANT.

155

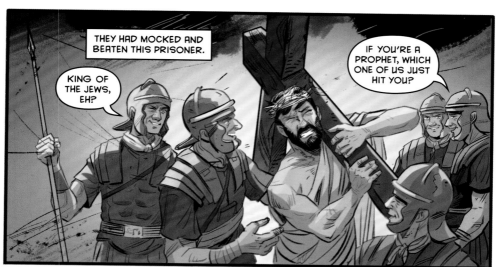

"GOD OF THE HEBREWS"? IT SEEMS TO ME NOW THAT OUR GOD IS FOR ALL PEOPLE. RIGHT, TEACHER?

TO AS MANY AS WILL RECEIVE THE LORD AS GOD, RACHEL. YES.

YESHUA MENTIONED JONAH ONCE. THE RELIGIOUS LEADERS WERE DEMANDING PROOF HE WAS FROM GOD. AND HE SAID . . .

JUST LIKE JONAH WAS IN THE BELLY OF THE BEAST FOR THREE DAYS, SO GOD'S SON WILL BE THREE DAYS AND NIGHTS IN THE HEART OF THE EARTH.

COULD IT BE? IT'S BEEN THREE DAYS SINCE HE WAS CRUCIFIED. HIS TOMB WAS EMPTY.

YESHUA, ALIVE AGAIN? I WANT TO BELIEVE IT, DEAR WIFE, BUT HOW?

I DUNNO. GOD DOES WHAT GOD WANTS. PEOPLE HAVE COME BACK TO LIFE BEFORE, YOU KNOW.

IT WOULD BE AMAZING TO SEE HIM. THEY SAY HE WAS A WONDERFUL TEACHER.

CHAPTER 7
THE SNAKE ON A STICK

171

DID GOD FREE US FROM SLAVERY SO WE COULD DIE IN THE DESERT?!

THERE'S NO BREAD HERE!

AND NO WATER EITHER!

THERE'S NOTHING TO EAT!

AND THIS MISERABLE FOOD IS THE WORST.

175

AH, FORGIVE ME, TEACHER, BUT IT REMINDS ME OF A STORY ABOUT YESHUA.

PLEASE, SISTER, TELL US.

A RELIGIOUS LEADER NAMED NICODEMUS CAME TO SEE YESHUA SECRETLY, AT NIGHT.

TEACHER, WE KNOW YOU ARE FROM GOD . . .

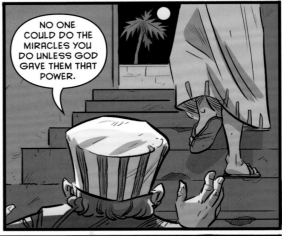

NO ONE COULD DO THE MIRACLES YOU DO UNLESS GOD GAVE THEM THAT POWER.

LISTEN, NO ONE CAN BE A PART OF GOD'S KINGDOM UNLESS THEY GET BORN AGAIN.

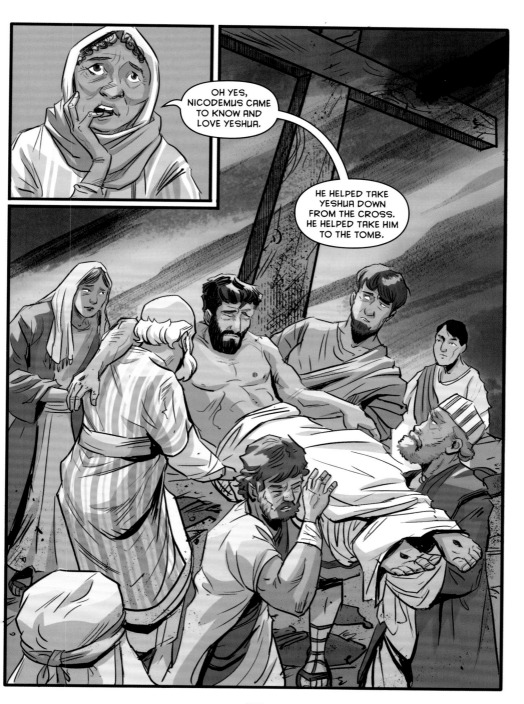

CHAPTER 8

A WIND AMONG THE BONES

THE LORD'S HAND WAS ON ME.

THE SOVEREIGN LORD LED ME BY THE SPIRIT.

IT WAS A VALLEY.

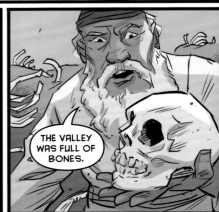

THE VALLEY WAS FULL OF BONES.

AND GOD ASKED ME, "SON OF MAN, CAN THESE DRY BONES COME TO LIFE AGAIN?"

AND THE LORD GAVE ME WORDS TO SAY TO THE BONES.

LISTEN UP, DRY BONES. THIS IS WHAT GOD SAYS: "I'M ABOUT TO BREATHE LIFE INTO YOU ONCE AGAIN."

THEN YOU WILL KNOW THAT GOD IS THE LORD OF ALL.

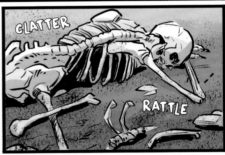

CLATTER

RATTLE

TENDONS, MUSCLES, AND SKIN CAME UPON THOSE BONES!

BUT THE BODIES HAD NO BREATH, NO SPIRIT—NO LONGER JUST BONES BUT STILL DEAD!

THERE WAS A WELL-KNOWN RELIGIOUS LEADER—I KNOW HIM MYSELF!—NAMED JAIRUS.

THERE WAS A WOMAN WHO HAD BEEN SICK WITH UNCONTROLLABLE BLEEDING FOR TWELVE YEARS.

HIS DAUGHTER WAS SICK . . . . SHE WAS DYING.

NO ONE COULD HELP HER. THE DOCTORS HAD TRIED EVERYTHING, BUT SHE ONLY GOT WORSE.

SO HE WENT TO FIND YESHUA, TO BEG HIM TO HEAL HER.

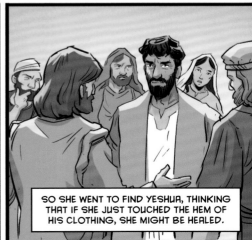

SO SHE WENT TO FIND YESHUA, THINKING THAT IF SHE JUST TOUCHED THE HEM OF HIS CLOTHING, SHE MIGHT BE HEALED.

MY LITTLE GIRL IS DYING. PLEASE COME. IF YOU PRAY FOR HER, I KNOW SHE WILL LIVE!

TAKE ME TO HER.

WHO TOUCHED ME?

IT COULD HAVE BEEN ANYONE, TEACHER. THE CROWD IS JOSTLING US CONSTANTLY.

NO, I FELT THE POWER GO OUT FROM ME. WHO TOUCHED ME?

TEACHER, MY DAUGHTER... WE MUST HURRY.

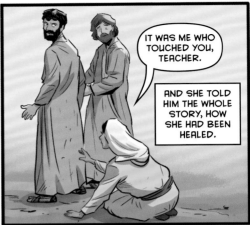

IT WAS ME WHO TOUCHED YOU, TEACHER.

AND SHE TOLD HIM THE WHOLE STORY, HOW SHE HAD BEEN HEALED.

I'M SORRY, SIR, BUT YOUR DAUGHTER... SHE'S DEAD.

NO!

COME HOME, SIR. NO NEED TO WAIT FOR THE TEACHER ANYMORE.

DAUGHTER, YOUR FAITH IN GOD HAS HEALED YOU. GO IN PEACE!

THANK YOU, SIR. OH, THANK YOU!

DON'T BE AFRAID, JAIRUS. JUST BELIEVE.

YESHUA'S MOM?

NO, MOSHE, ANOTHER MARY!

MARTHA.

MARY.

AND LAZARUS.

LAZARUS FELL ILL— DEATHLY ILL.

LET'S SEND FOR YESHUA.

HE'S HEALED SO MANY PEOPLE.... OF COURSE HE CAN HEAL LAZARUS.

YESHUA, SIR, I HAVE A MESSAGE: "LAZARUS, WHOM YOU LOVE, IS DYING. PLEASE COME AT ONCE."

BUT YESHUA DID NOT GO.

YOUR BROTHER WILL LIVE AGAIN.

YES, I KNOW GOD WILL BRING US ALL TO LIFE AGAIN IN THE END, AT THE RESURRECTION.

I AM THE RESURRECTION AND THE LIFE. THOSE WHO BELIEVE IN ME LIVE, EVEN IF THEY DIE. THOSE WHO LIVE IN ME AND BELIEVE WILL NEVER DIE.

DO YOU BELIEVE, MARTHA?

YES, LORD. I BELIEVE YOU ARE THE MESSIAH, THE SAVIOR OF THE WORLD, GOD'S SON WHO WAS SENT TO US.

MARTHA RAN TO TELL HER SISTER, "THE TEACHER IS HERE, AND HE'S ASKING TO SEE YOU."

MARY WENT TO HIM AT ONCE, ALONG WITH MANY OF HER FRIENDS WHO WERE MOURNING WITH HER.

WHEN HE SAW MARY AND ALL THE OTHERS WHO LOVED LAZARUS CRYING, YESHUA WAS DEEPLY MOVED AND TROUBLED.

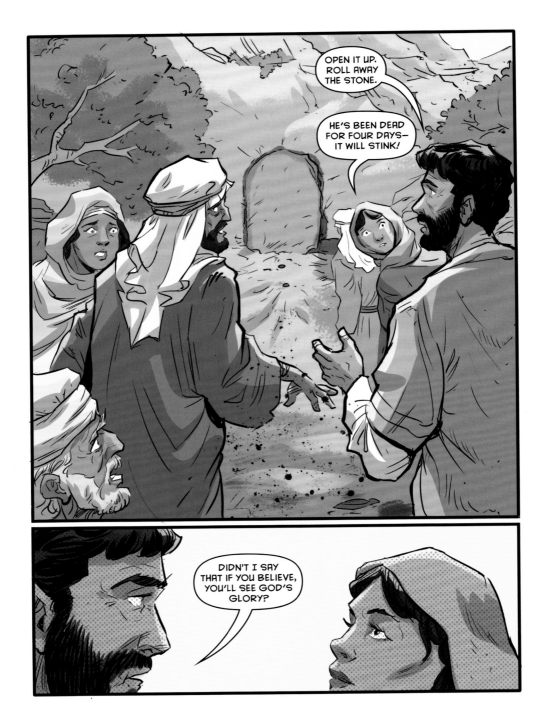

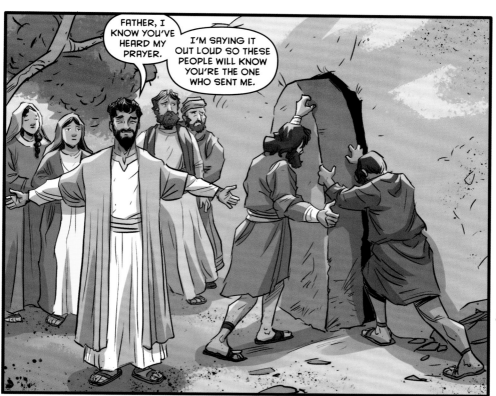

HOW DO YOU KNOW LAZARUS'S BODY WASN'T STOLEN?
WASN'T HIS TOMB EMPTY TOO?
PEOPLE SAW HIM!
THIS MORNING SOME WOMEN WENT TO PUT SPICES ON YESHUA'S BODY, BUT THE TOMB WAS OPEN. THEY SAID AN ANGEL WAS THERE.
WHY ARE YOU LOOKING FOR THE LIVING IN A CEMETERY?
DO YOU BELIEVE THEM, MIRIAM?
RACHEL . . .
I WAS ONE OF THEM.
MIRIAM! TELL US THE REST OF THE STORY!

CHAPTER 9

BURNING

A FEW NIGHTS AGO—THE NIGHT WHEN YESHUA WAS BETRAYED—THERE WAS NO SERVANT TO WASH THEIR FEET.

FEET GET PRETTY DIRTY WHEN YOU WEAR SANDALS ALL THE TIME. THAT'S WHAT MY MOM SAYS ANYWAY.

EVERYONE WAS TIRED AND DIRTY, AND THERE WAS NO ONE TO REFRESH THEM BEFORE THE MEAL.

SO YESHUA STRIPPED TO HIS TUNIC . . .

AND WASHED THE FEET OF HIS FOLLOWERS.

AND HE SAID TO THEM . . .

NOW THAT I, YOUR TEACHER, HAVE SERVED YOU . . .

YOU SHOULD SERVE EACH OTHER.

I'VE GIVEN YOU AN EXAMPLE TO FOLLOW.

AND WHAT DID HE SAY AT THE MEAL, HUSBAND?

IT SEEMS SO IMPORTANT NOW!

HE PRAYED A BLESSING OVER THE MEAL AND THEN . . .

EAT THIS. IT'S MY BODY, BROKEN FOR YOU.

DRINK THIS. IT'S MY BLOOD, SPILLED OUT FOR YOU.

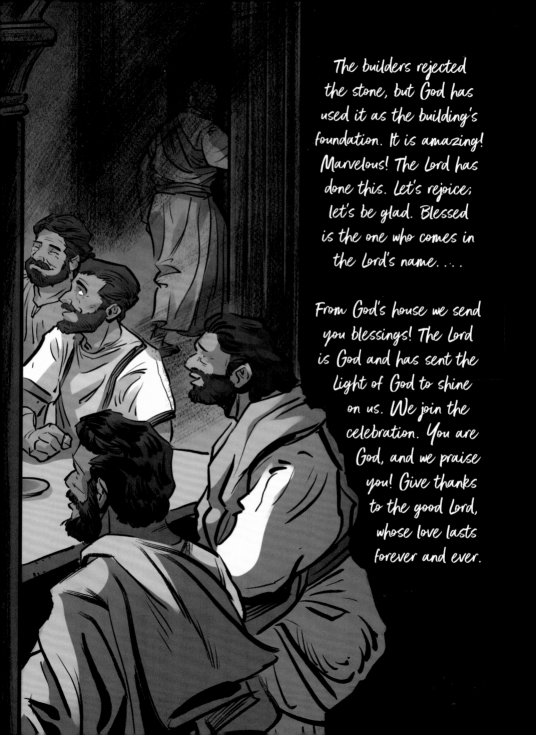

The builders rejected the stone, but God has used it as the building's foundation. It is amazing! Marvelous! The Lord has done this. Let's rejoice; let's be glad. Blessed is the one who comes in the Lord's name. . . .

From God's house we send you blessings! The Lord is God and has sent the light of God to shine on us. We join the celebration. You are God, and we praise you! Give thanks to the good Lord, whose love lasts forever and ever.

FATHER GOD, FORGIVE THEM! THEY HAVE NO IDEA WHAT THEY'RE DOING!

SOME MOCKED HIM.

CALL THE ANGELS TO SAVE YOU!

AREN'T YOU A KING?

COMMAND YOUR ARMIES TO TAKE YOU DOWN!

JOHN . . .

TAKE CARE OF MY MOTHER.

HE WAS THIRSTY.

AT ABOUT THREE IN THE AFTERNOON . . .

IT'S FINISHED.

FATHER, I GIVE MY SPIRIT INTO YOUR HANDS.

WE COMFORTED EACH OTHER AS WELL AS WE COULD.

AND SATURDAY NIGHT I WENT WITH TWO OF THE OTHER WOMEN TO BUY SPICES AT THE MARKET.

WE HADN'T EVEN PREPARED YESHUA'S BODY FOR BURIAL YET.

THE ROMANS SENT SOLDIERS TO PROTECT THE TOMB.

EARLY SUNDAY MORNING, JUST AFTER SUNRISE, SOME OF US WENT TO THE TOMB.

HOW WILL WE ROLL THE STONE AWAY? IT'S TOO HEAVY.

THE STONE IS GONE!

AND THE GUARDS WERE GONE TOO! BUT INSIDE . . .

DIDN'T THE SAVIOR OF THE WORLD HAVE TO SUFFER ALL OF THIS AND THEN ENTER INTO HIS GLORY?

NOT AT ALL.

DON'T YOU SEE? YESHUA HUMBLED HIMSELF AND OBEYED GOD ALL THE WAY TO DEATH.

AND NOW AT HIS NAME EVERY KNEE WILL BOW—IN HEAVEN, ON EARTH, AND UNDER THE EARTH—AND EVERY TONGUE CONFESS THAT YESHUA, SAVIOR OF THE WORLD, IS LORD, TO THE GLORY OF GOD THE FATHER.

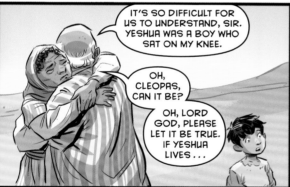

IT'S SO DIFFICULT FOR US TO UNDERSTAND, SIR. YESHUA WAS A BOY WHO SAT ON MY KNEE.

OH, CLEOPAS, CAN IT BE?

OH, LORD GOD, PLEASE LET IT BE TRUE. IF YESHUA LIVES . . .

HEY! THERE'S MOM AND DAD!

MOSHE!

RACHEL!

MIRIAM!

CLEOPAS!

THANK YOU FOR WALKING WITH THE CHILDREN.

BUT I WAS HOPING FOR ONE MORE STORY!

I WAS HOPING FOR THREE OR FOUR.

YOU TWO SAY GOODBYE TO THE TEACHER.

WE'LL STALL YOUR PARENTS FOR A FEW MINUTES.

ONE MORE STORY, EH?

WELL, WHAT SHALL IT BE?

I KNOW WHO YOU ARE. YOU'VE NEVER SAID YOUR NAME, BUT—

WHY DOESN'T ANYTHING COOL EVER HAPPEN TO ME?

WHAT DO YOU MEAN, MOSHE?

I NEVER GET TO CROSS THE RED SEA OR SEND A PLAGUE OR KILL YOUTHS WITH BEARS.

I NEVER EVEN GOT TO SEE YESHUA DO A MIRACLE.

LIKE FEEDING EVERYONE—I WANT TO EAT A MIRACLE FISH.

ONE DAY MARTHA HOSTED YESHUA TO TEACH, AND AS ALWAYS, SHE DID AN AMAZING JOB: THERE WAS BREAD AND FISH AND LAMB AND OLIVES AND CHEESE.

OH! THE BREAD IS BURNING!

I CAN'T DO EVERYTHING ALL AT ONCE.

MARY SAT AT YESHUA'S FEET, LISTENING TO HIM TEACH.

CHAPTER 10

HEARTS AFLAME

WELCOME TO OUR HOME!

SIT, SIT!

BE REFRESHED, GOOD SIR.

IT HAS BEEN A LONG JOURNEY.

FRIEND, WILL YOU PRAY THE BLESSING?

IT WOULD BE MY PLEASURE.

YESHUA?

IS IT REALLY YOU?

THAT'S IMPOSSIBLE!

BUT MARY FROM MAGDALA . . . SHE SAID SHE SAW HIM THIS MORNING!

HE'S GONE!

WHERE IS HE?

I CAN'T BELIEVE THIS.

I CAN'T BELIEVE THIS, BUT I DO. WE HAVE TO GO TELL THE OTHERS.

OF COURSE. OF COURSE, YOU'RE RIGHT!

Now when you read the holy words, you will see what is written: that the Savior of the world had to suffer, that he would rise from the dead on the third day, and that the whole world would be told that if they turn away from doing the wrong thing and toward God, they will be forgiven. And this good news WILL BE TOLD to everyone, starting right here in Jerusalem. You saw all this. You heard all this. My Father promised to send you someone. So stay here, in this city, until God's power comes down on you like a dove, like holy fire.